WHISPERS FROM THE EARTH

'Teaching stories are a part of many traditions. Jesus used them. Native Americans passed their teaching stories from generation to generation. Sufi stories make us both think and smile. Taz Thornton's delightful book *Whispers from the Earth* is a goldmine of stories for teachers, motivational speakers, healers and clergymen — regardless of who they are targeting. Thornton's easy writing style also makes this marvellous resource a pleasure to read, just for its entertainment value. I very much enjoyed it.'
Tolly Burkan

'It is always a pleasure and something of a revelation to read a new book by a great spiritual teacher like Taz Thornton. She has been gifted with two of the most important qualities a true teacher can possess – integrity and genuine insight. I discover something new about the material and the invisible world every time I am privileged to read something she has written and I can honestly say that I gain a new perspective on life from her work that few in the esoteric tradition can offer.'
Paul Roland, author of *I Remember Dying* (Foulsham) and *Meditation Solutions* (Hamlyn)

'*Whispers of the Earth* is filled with inspiring stories that help to light our way as we follow our soul's journey and life adventure. Taz Thorton is a brilliant and gifted storyteller!'
Sandra Ingerman, MA author of *Walking in Light: the Everyday Empowerment of Shamanic Life*

'Thank you for the stories I feel much creative 'shooting' occurring here. I think the project you are working on is very worthwhile and important for us all at this time.

'One root of the word 'story' is 'storehouse' i.e. stories are storehouses of knowledge for the deep imagination and those stories that survive through the generations have great truths within them that can serve as guidance and nourishment for our inner journeys. I love the passion and commitment you have to this work and I look forward to re-reading the stories you have sent me for my own pleasure.'
Howard Malpas, Warrior in the Heart Foundation

'Throughout history stories have been a crucial means of learning and growing. They have been told around hearths all over the earth since ancient times, keeping the wisdom teachings alive, and passing on the knowledge of land and ancestors. Taz Thornton has written and collated new stories, based in these lands, that contribute to keeping an old tradition alive and well.'
Chris Lüttichau, founder of Northern Drum Shamanic Centre and author of *Animal Spirit Guides: Discover your power animal and the shamanic path*

Whispers from the Earth

Teaching stories from the ancestors,
beautifully woven for today's
spiritual seekers

Whispers from the Earth

Teaching stories from the ancestors, beautifully woven for today's spiritual seekers

Taz Thornton

MOON
BOOKS

Winchester, UK
Washington, USA

First published by Moon Books, 2016
Moon Books is an imprint of John Hunt Publishing Ltd., Laurel House, Station Approach,
Alresford, Hants, SO24 9JH, UK
office1@jhpbooks.net
www.johnhuntpublishing.com
www.moon-books.net

For distributor details and how to order please visit the 'Ordering' section on our website.

Text copyright: Taz Thornton 2015

ISBN: 978 1 78279 382 3
Library of Congress Control Number: 2015952165

A CIP catalogue record for this book is available from the British Library.

Design: Stuart Davies

Printed and bound by CPI Group (UK) Ltd, Croydon, CR0 4YY, UK

We operate a distinctive and ethical publishing philosophy in all
areas of our business, from our global network of authors to
production and worldwide distribution.

CONTENTS

Foreword

When I was asked to write this foreword for Taz's first book, *Whispers from the Earth*, I was deeply humbled and truly delighted.

Taz may be my wife, my lover and my best friend but, above all, she is a true walker between the worlds in every sense. Her dry, take-no-nonsense, straight talking approach may ruffle feathers from time to time, but only when those feathers are ready to be ruffled, even if the owner of said feathers has yet to acknowledge it.

To see her work, guided by her spirit teachers and guides, in whatever setting – from shamanic and other spiritual gatherings to festivals, shows, business exhibitions and network meetings is a beautiful thing and I feel truly blessed to have her by my side through life's journey.

Meet Taz and I believe you are truly touched by spirit, sometimes in the most unlikely, but most incredibly powerful, of ways. These stories will also touch you when you let them in.

That's why I make no apologies for these words of love, appreciation and gratitude as they come from the heart and Taz, as I'm sure many of her tribe will attest to, is all about heart as is this, her first creation as a published author.

Whispers from the Earth is a true labour of love and a beautiful collection of teachings channelled from spirit and brought together with open hearts by some of the wonderful people who have walked and continue to walk this incredible path with her.

Approach this book with an open heart and mind and let its powerful words wash over you so your soul may absorb what's needed for you at this time and every time you reconnect and touch its pages.

Love comes in many forms and in these pages it shines bright. Even after 17 years together there are never enough words to express the love I have and will always have for Taz and how proud of her I am, so I'll keep it simple.

Love always,
Asha
x8

Introduction

For many years, I've been fascinated by teaching stories from across the globe. Fables, legends, parables, myths…whatever term is used, they're often full of rich lessons if we only search for them.

One of the greatest teachers on my spiritual path loved relaying these teaching tales from his time learning direct from elders in the Americas – stories of how Raven stole the sun, Jumping Mouse and many others became a high point of our workshops, as we gathered around the fire, eager to listen and learn. I'll always remember him explaining how the wise people of the village would tell these stories to groups of children, and how the messages always hit exactly where they needed to; he called this 'shooting' someone with a story.

Since then, I've come across many wonderful storytellers, yet none seemed to be telling the stories of our own lands. Sure, there are European 'fairytales' to fall back on (which all hold hidden threads of truth if we're willing to search for them), but what about stories from our own ancient past? What of our own beautiful tapestry? What of all those beautiful teachings held by the ancestors of our own lands?

It was after listening, enthralled, to a wonderful bard that I really felt the pull from Spirit to delve further. I felt the ancestor spirits tugging at my sleeve – and at my heart – to quest for our own parables…and that's where my real adventure began.

It began with the land – for the lands we tread hold the bones and the teeth of the ancestors; through a series of meditations, I began to be gifted with some of the most beautifully woven tales I'd ever heard. Later, working with some of my spiritual development students, we widened the project, all connecting with the spirits of times past and all channelling amazing life lessons, told through wonderful stories. Clearly, the ancestors were pleased that finally, after hundreds of years, new storyweavers were stepping forward, respectfully and with open hearts, to carry these teachings forward to new generations.

What I've found most amazing is that, despite the age of these tales, their teachings are perfect for modern day. And there are still plenty to be sourced. In these pages, I'll share meditations and teachings to help you source your own teaching stories from the earth, as well as a collection of wonderful tales already told to me, direct from the spirits of our ancestors.

Read on, but remember that the task of a storyweaver is not merely to seek, but to help these tales find their mark on today's world, to carry them to new generations and, hopefully, to 'shoot' all who need their teachings with wisdom, love and adventure.

Chapter 1

Beginning the Story

There are many ways to get into the flow of storytelling and, later in this book, I'll be gifting you with plenty of ideas to help you work with spirit to channel some beautiful tales. Like any exercise, it's always good to begin with a warm-up, and story-weaving is no different – we need to start toning our 'bardic muscles' with some gentle introductory work. In this way, we can encourage our creativity to flow and not get stuck in trying to force a story onto the page, which simply creates a head/heart disconnect. Heart, you see, is far more important than head in storyweaving – we're not trying to invent teaching tales to fit a particular subject, as one might in NLP practices but, rather, allowing the words to flow through us, bringing all kinds of teachings with them as they grow. Sometimes, when channelling a story, the teachings are immediately obvious but, in many cases, I've re-read a channelled story years later and discovered a whole batch of new teachings; they really do deliver to us precisely what we need at the time – even if we weren't aware of our requirement!

So, how might we get into the flow of storyweaving? Well, one way might be to begin with something familiar to us and tap into our creativity to breathe new life into it. Allow yourself to think back to your favourite childhood fairytale, whatever that might be, and try to remember what so enthralled you about it. Looking back now, through the eyes of an adult, what teachings did it hold for you, and how might you be able to retell that story?

Some years ago, I had the pleasure of meeting Canadian storyteller and harpist Jeff Stockton at a gathering. Jeff enthralled us all with a beautiful Celtic tale, before inviting us all to work in groups, retelling familiar stories to each other to bring forth their teachings. Sitting out in the sunshine that day, I listened to a retelling of Rumpelstiltskin and the Tale of Taliesin; I chose to tell the old story of the two wolves and, as I wove together the words, creating the powerful teaching that had once hit me right between the eyes, it became evident that neither of my friends had heard the story before, and the power of the retelling suddenly filled my gut. You see, the thing about teaching stories is that they carry many lessons; often, the subtler teachings are hidden deep, deftly woven 'tween the words, yet always finding their prey and pouncing, their lessons carrying deep into the soul of the eager listener. Whichever teaching an individual needs is heard and absorbed right into the heart – that's why one of my old shamanic teachers used to refer to 'shooting' people with a story. Until now, however, I'd never told a traditional teaching story to people who hadn't heard it before. I watched the emotions play out on their faces as the story unfurled, saw the teachings hit their mark, and their smiles as they began to understand. And then…then, I began to wonder. I began to hear that whisper on the breeze, feel that familiar tug on my heart that would only become stronger if I tried to resist. It called my name, and I knew exactly who the words belonged to…this particular ancestor spirit has never pulled any punches with me. What she wants, she generally gets, and this was to be no exception.

'There are plenty more where this came from,' came the voice. 'We're holding them for you. The stories from your own lands. We hid them. We're waiting to share them again…' and then, as if by magic, the hidden teachings meant for my heart began to make sense; I realised little clues had been slipped into conversations throughout the day, I remembered some of the signs I'd seen in nature and how they all carried their own stories, and the idea for this book began to take shape. Just moments earlier, chatting with my storytelling pals, we'd touched on those teachings from our own lands being hidden in fairytales, put there to keep them safe when our own indigenous spirituality was being stamped out. We'd chatted about myths and legends, about the glimpses of our ancient spirituality still visible in things we take for granted...the chocolate Easter bunnies bearing a striking resemblance to sacred hares, the unproven suggestions of the dark origins of the Easter egg hunt, a magical past, assumed to be fiction, hiding in European fairy tales. I remembered a fascination with the Brothers Grimm as a child, Hans Christian Andersen...could these tales really carry glimpses of the truth, an essence of our past? But what of the stories from ancient Britain? Where were they? I wanted to hear them now, wanted to learn, to explore...and then came that whisper again, deep within my chest: 'They're here. We have them. We're waiting...'

Chapter 2

The Stories

Through the following pages of this book, you'll find a collection of stories channelled from the earth, from the ancestors. Unless otherwise stated, each of these tales has been channelled and re-written by me, though there is a selection of wonderful stories channelled by some of my equally wonderful students towards the end of the book.

What counts as an ancestor? Well, I'm not here to give you definitive answers – my task is merely to open a doorway and invite you to walk through. Ancestor – though on the face of it such a simple word – can be viewed in so many ways; we might think of ancestors as members of our long departed blood or spirit lines who once trod these lands as we do now. Some of you might think of ancestors as all those ancient, all-knowing beings who might be willing to share their wisdom with us – the fae, the elementals, angelic beings, star people...who knows? Some might even think about the ancestors yet to come for, if time is not really linear, we are already ancestors ourselves. For the purposes of this book though – at least for the stories channelled by me – the ancestors fall into those first two brackets: spirits of our ancient past and spirits of the land.

Sometimes, these stories have downloaded (because that's the best word I can find in modern language to describe what happens – it's like a huge, sudden blast of beautiful words, pictures, sounds, moving images, smells and senses dropped into my head and heart) hard and fast, and sometimes they've gradually wended their way into my subconscious, perhaps during meditation, or a medicine walk, before spilling beautifully out onto the page and coming to life as a story. Sometimes the story has been told to me; a spoken voice weaving the tale into being, as if listening to a real, live storyweaver. Sometimes, I have seen the words and images on an otherworldly page offered to me by one of my trusted guides, and sometimes I have watched the story play out in my mind's eye – or during a shamanic journey or astral adventure – and have then done my best to weave the adventure into words for you.

Some of these stories may be suitable for you to pass on to your children, and to your children's children, and to the children who have yet to come, and some are more suitable for adults. Make no mistake – although some of the stories here may be well received by youngsters, this is not a children's book, and I would urge you to read it cover to cover before deciding who to pass it on to, or who to gift a copy to; follow your heart and your gut instinct and you won't go far wrong.

In order to source these teaching stories, I have been out in nature, visited ancient sites, talked to the tree folk and rock people and been gifted some of the most beautiful teachings to share. Some of the lessons are screamingly obvious, some more subtle – and whichever teachings you find, the ones you notice – the ones that land in your heart – will absolutely be the ones you need.

Before going further, what I will say is this: whether you choose to believe these stories have been gifted by spirits and energy beings, or whether you choose to believe they have been borne from my imagination matters not. What *does* matter is how much you enjoy them, how much they speak to you and how much you learn from them. Anything over and above that is gravy.

And so, without further delay, on to the stories...

Why Pheasant's Face is Red

Many years ago, in a time long before you and I were even thought of, Great Spirit gifted all the animals and birds with special powers.

To the frogs he gave a sticky tongue with which to catch their food and powerful legs with which to leap great distances; to the ants he gave strength with which to carry great bounties to the rest of the colony; to the deer he gave great heart with which to carry their gentle strength and to bear he gave knowledge of healing plants and roots to use in medicine.

Every creature, great and small, was granted some divine power, skill or armour to take forth into the great teachings of the world.

Pheasant was gifted with a beautiful coat of reds, oranges and greens; resplendent and as a warning for others not to eat him. As well as this glorious rainbow jacket, Pheasant was granted wings with which to escape from predators who might allow their hunger to cloud their judgement.

But Pheasant grew lazy. Awed by his beauty, he spent days preening and gazing at his reflection. Before long, Pheasant grew fat and beating his wings to float into the air became far too much effort.

Gradually, Pheasant's predators grew wise to the inactivity of he and his kin and began to pounce until, over time, his brightly coloured coat stopped being seen as a warning and, instead, became seen as a shining beacon signalling dinner time! Other creatures urged Pheasant to flap his wings and fly away, but Pheasant always refused.

'Why has Great Spirit cursed me so?' he would cry. 'When I was plain and unnoticed nobody bothered me and I lived my life in peace.'

'But Pheasant,' came the reply, 'Great Spirit has gifted you with such beauty *and* the ability to soar like the eagles. Anyone would be eternally grateful for such wonderful powers.' Pheasant would always shake his head, feebly lift his wings against his plump body and sigh. 'It's no use. These things are useless. I am cursed.'

One day, Great Spirit himself came down to speak to Pheasant. 'My child, why do you sit and wait to be eaten instead of using the gifts I have given you?' he asked.

Pheasant scowled. 'You call these gifts? Predators see me from miles around because of these stupid colours and these wings are too heavy for me to lift!'

Great Spirit shook his head. 'Pheasant, it is your own vanity that has rendered you inactive. It is not your wings that are too heavy, but your ego.'

Feeling wounded by the Creator's words, Pheasant became angry. 'You do not understand what it's like! If you could only experience the pain I go through every day, maybe you would have greater sympathy for the mess you've landed me in.' Great Spirit tried again. 'Dear Pheasant, alongside your beauty, I have given you the ability to make good your situation. You have only to believe in yourself, to have faith in the divine power of nature, and you will be able to fly. The more you move your wings, the lighter you will become, and the higher you soar, the more insight you will gain.'

Pheasant's face grew redder and redder as his anger took hold. He let out a cry: 'Because of you and your stupid gifts, my kin are dying out. Very soon, there will be only me left, with my beautiful feathers and my useless body. You have done this. I should just die now and get it all over with!'

Great Spirit reached forward and touched Pheasant's heart. His plumage instantly turned brown from the neck down but, still filled with rage, Pheasant's face remained bright red.

'Do not worry about your kinfolk,' the Creator spoke gently. 'I will see to it that your clan is always plentiful, but the choice between victim and warrior will always be yours.'

To this day, Pheasant still resists using his wings and frequently runs into the path of his predators instead of choosing to escape into the air. It is said that Pheasant's face will remain an angry red until the day he truly embraces the call of the sky.

The Great Boy Warrior

Many years ago, in a faraway tribe, lived a young boy. He was the only one of his age group in the village – too old to play with the children, but too young to be considered a hunter, gatherer or warrior like his older brothers and cousins.

Day after day, the boy would kick around at the edges of the village, watching as his brothers and their friends went out on the hunt and returned with rich bounties to sustain the men, women and children. Day after day, the boy would call after them and plead with them to take him along. 'Stay in the village,' always came the reply. 'You're too young and immature to join us menfolk!'

The boy's mother tried her best to include him in village life, but he did not want to hang around baking bread with the women, herding the cattle or tending the old folk, no matter the rich teachings his mother promised the experiences would bring. In the evenings, the boy would feel even more miserable and alone. The menfolk would sit in circle around the fire, talking village business and sharing stories of hunting, visits to outlying settlements and discussing messages from spirit, but the boy was not allowed to join in, for he was too young for such gatherings. He had been invited to sit with the womenfolk many times, but he did not like the way they teased him about the young girls in the village and guessed which one he might take as his wife one day. So, he chose to skulk around in the shadows, kicking up dirt at the edges of the fire site and listening to all he could from the menfolk gathered there. Sometimes, they'd spot him and tell him to go back to his mother, but every now and then, he managed to sit quietly, unnoticed until the flames died down and the embers began to glow deep red.

One day, the boy woke from a brilliant dream: he dreamed he brought down a great red deer with his hunting knife and was the hero of the village, having single-handedly brought in enough food to sustain them for some time.

'This is it!' he exclaimed. 'This dream was a message from Spirit. It is *my* time now and time I was seen as a man!' Gathering himself, the boy got up, washed, ate and set out to visit the village elder and chief.

At the door of the chief's hut, the boy waited for a few moments before hearing a voice beckoning him inside. The hut smelled of smoke and warmth, and the chief nodded to the boy and motioned for him to speak.

'It's time you and all the village saw me as a man,' said the boy.

The chief raised a brow, but the boy continued.

'Spirit came to me in a dream last night. I brought back a huge red deer for the village...the biggest deer I'd ever seen! This is a message from Spirit, telling you all that I am as fine a huntsman as you ever did see, and that you are withholding great bounty from the tribe by not seeing me as a man or allowing me to hunt.'

All this time, the great chief said nothing, his eyes cast down as he listened to the boy's wavering words. The boy waited and, finally, the chief spoke: 'How can you be so sure of the dream's meaning?' he asked. 'You are not our seer, and you did not attend her to learn when the opportunity arose.'

The boy thought for a second. 'Because I am meant for greater things,' he said. 'That is what the dream meant. How can I hunt such magnificent game if I spend my days tending to our old folk? That's why spirit sent me the dream! To show you! To show everyone!'

The chief threw some herbs into the fire and thought. 'If it was *my* dream, I'd be wondering if there could be another meaning. The dream weavers do not always speak arrow straight. Perhaps the great deer represents something else you need to slay...'

'No!' the boy interrupted. 'It was MY dream. I KNOW what it means. I cannot believe you are being so blind!'

The old chief nodded and looked the boy in the eye. 'You are right. Your brain is much younger than mine, of course, so it works much more swiftly.'

The boy stood up straighter, eyes widening at the chief's words. He nodded.

'If you are such a great huntsman,' said the chief, 'you will need to prove it to all the menfolk, not just me. We will need to see how quickly that young mind of yours works and whether your feet can keep up with it. You'll need to demonstrate heart, speed and good sportsmanship.'

'That will be easy,' said the boy.

Again, the chief nodded. 'Come to the fire when the moon reaches her highest point. Demonstrate these abilities and show us the man you claim to be. We will be waiting.'

For the rest of the day, the boy puffed out his chest and walked tall. He practised running, leaping, throwing, tumbling and everything else he could think of to show the tribesmen. He told his mother to prepare a feast in his honour, for tonight he would be recognised as a man and, by the will of Spirit, the greatest hunter the village had ever known. His mother smiled and went about her tasks.

That night, when the moon reached her highest point, the boy made his way to the men's circle. Stepping out from the shadows, he announced his arrival and strode towards the fire; the menfolk stepped back to let him through.

Silence fell as the chief spoke: 'This young man came to see me today. He says Spirit visited him in the night and told him to let us all know that he is our greatest hunter. In his dream, the boy took down a giant red deer and we feasted on its flesh for weeks, whilst our women folk made clothes and bedding from its hide. If the boy's interpretation of the dream is true, then we have been foolish in seeing him merely as a child.'

The boy turned full circle, looking at each of the men in turn, his eyes hard to prove his maturity, before turning his attention back to the chief. 'I am ready,' he said, 'to show you my great, Spirit-given skills.'

With that, the chief reached into the fire with two lengths of antler and brought out a red hot coal. Without speaking, he flung the glowing stone towards the boy, who immediately reached out and caught it with his bare hands.

Screaming in pain, the boy dropped the coal and began to blow on his hand. Tears streaming, he yelled at the chief: 'You STUPID old man! Why would you do that! I am a strong, fast hunter, but my skin will still melt!'

'You said your brain was swifter than mine,' the chief replied, 'that you were quick witted, strong of heart and a good sportsman...'

'I AM ALL OF THOSE,' yelled the boy, flinging his hand around in the air in an effort to cool it. 'I was quick enough to catch your stupid coal!'

The chief smiled. 'A good hunter knows when to dodge something dangerous. A good sportsman knows how to react to a poorly played game. A good man, with a strong heart, knows humility. Perhaps the great deer, sent by spirit, represented something else after all.'

The Girl Who Was Different and the Wasp King

Many years ago, in a village not too far from here, there lived a young girl. Growing up, all the other kids in the village decided she was different. Nobody now remembers why she seemed so different then – maybe she wore the wrong clothes, maybe she loved the wrong people, maybe she knew too much and was old before her time. Whatever the reason, it doesn't matter now; it's not important to the story.

Feeling isolated and alone, the girl spent lots of time on her own; she'd create little projects for herself and get really absorbed in them: why the grass was green, how the wild birds spoke to each other and knew to fly in flocks, how the ant people could carry things so much bigger than them... She'd occupy herself with all kinds of different questions and quest for the answers. It kept her busy and it stopped her thinking about the other kids in the village too much.

Every so often, though, the village kids would get bored and decide to pick on the girl who was different. Because so many years have passed, we'll probably never really know the truth about why they did this...maybe they were scared of her, maybe they overheard their parents saying unkind things about her, or maybe they were a bit curious – maybe even jealous – about her deep insight into the magic of Mother Nature. Whatever the reason...it doesn't really matter.

What does matter is that no matter how much the girl tried to keep herself busy, no matter how much she pleaded with the other children to leave her alone, or to stop bullying her, they just wouldn't listen. They'd move into her personal space, make cruel jibes, sometimes even kick out and ruin things she'd been making, or stamp out the images she'd drawn in the earth.

One day, after a particularly vicious incident (well, it felt vicious to the girl...to you and I, as grownups, it probably just looked like children being children...), the girl got so upset she stood and ran as fast as her legs would carry her. She ran and ran and ran and ran, until she became aware of blurry black shapes darting about through her tears, until she heard buzzing sounds and until she felt a sharp pain, just above the centre of her brow – the place you and I might describe as the shamanic eye.

'Leave me alone!' cried the girl who was different. 'You're just as bad as they are! Please, don't sting me anymore!'

The wasp king smiled – at least, if insects could smile, he would have done.

'Dear one,' he said gently, 'we are nothing like the children in your village. All we want to do is go about our business...whether we're eating sweet nectar, spreading pollen as we go, or protecting our nest. It was *you* who came stumbling into *our* space – not the other way around! *You* disturbed *us*. We are simply protecting ourselves – and each other.'

The girl thought for a moment. Had she really gone trampling into their sacred space, just as the village children had trampled over hers so many times? And even if she had, she certainly hadn't meant to harm them. Why did they choose to sting her so?

As if hearing her thoughts, the wasp king spoke again. 'We are not intentionally cruel,' he explained, 'but people do fear us, and those who do not fear us usually respect our space.'

'Perhaps people fear you because they don't understand you,' said the girl. 'You seem so willing to sting us for no reason! And you serve no real purpose, as far as I can see.'

The wasp king shook his head: 'For one so gifted, you're not too bright when you're feeling attacked...'

As he began to fly into the distance, he called back over his wings: 'Our purpose is to teach you humans the importance of boundaries. We don't sting very often, but the *fear* of our sting means people leave us alone!'

The next day, when the girl woke up, she rubbed the space

where she'd been stung and – do you know what happened next? There was no pain. Not even a red mark to prove her ordeal. From that day forth, though, she chose to stand her ground instead of running away from the other children. She held her space well, planting her feet and looking them square in the eye. Her newfound confidence scared some of them away, yet some of the wiser children grew to respect her and even took time out to get to know her a little more.

The girl who was different began to make friends and, do you know, she never did need to use her sting!

Faerietale of the British Isles

Many years ago, in a time before books, before paper, before even churches, human beings and the fae lived harmoniously, as allies on Mother Earth.

Faeries, pixies, imps, dryads, sylphs – even gnomes – were commonplace, and could often be seen deep in conversation with their human companions. We would talk together, eat together, dance together, everything you would expect firm friends to do. The faefolk would share their magics with us for the common good, and us humans would share our strength with them because, magical creatures aside, we were the largest and mightiest of the people-shaped beings.

Way back then, all kinds of animals now extinct to British shores also shared the land with us. The faefolk had wonderful relationships with these species, riding on the backs of the wolves and working with the bears to create fabulous healing potions and remedies with the roots they'd dig up.

For many, many years – more years than you or I could count – the humans and the fae lived as one, in harmony with the bears, the wolves, the wild boar, unicorns, griffins and dragons, and they were happy times, filled with joy and laughter.

Over time, though, we humans began to grow arrogant. Despite the wonderful magics and gentle energies of the faeriefolk, we humankind allowed our comparative brute strength to go to our heads, trampling over the plant life and vegetation, pulling down trees and using our might to try to force our fae kin into using their magics for entertainment, or to control the will of nature.

At first, our fae brethren tried to reason with us, but our self-proclaimed power, and the ego that bred within us, corrupted our spirits and made us arrogant and unforgiving. 'Why should we yield to these tiny folk when the Great Shaper gave us such might?' we argued. 'We are bigger than you, stronger than you, so we're in charge here,' we said.

Still, even as humans captured the fire faeries and forced them to light our way, held the elvish folk slaves and made them use their magical swords and bows to clear paths for us, and coerced the sylphs to sing for us against their will, the fae held onto the hope that one day soon we'd realise our mistake and humbly realign ourselves with nature, allowing us all to live in harmony once more.

It was when the killing began that the fae really withdrew their support from us. First, we wiped out the unicorns, the griffins, the dragons and all beings now described as 'mythical' – and, worse still, we held the hunters aloft as heroes. When that was done, we began to wipe out our animal helpers – bears and wolves eventually disappeared from our lands, and we began to hunt others almost to the point of extinction. It was this bloodshed that finally, ultimately, drove our fae cousins underground and saw them cut off any contact with humankind.

Of course, when that happened, all those wonderful magics disappeared. Back then, we humans never really understood the true power of the fae, that those held captive or mistreated could have escaped, or turned their magics on us at any time, but suffered our arrogance and corruption out of love and hope for us. And when the fae truly withdrew support, when they could no longer bear to face their disappointment in all we'd become, their sadness and grief from all we'd destroyed, we realised just how much we'd come to rely on them. No more magics to treat our ills, heal our wounds, boost our feasts or entertain and teach our children. But still, our arrogance and thirst for power prevented us from mourning our loss, or accepting our stupidity, or trying to make amends. Instead, we invented colourful stories to cover our tracks, of dragons who preyed on innocent villagers, or mermaids who lured sailors to their deaths, of will-o'-the-wisps who wreaked havoc across the moors and fens. Over time, the stories came to be dismissed as nothing but folk tales, and the faeries and nature spirits came to be seen as fictional beings, made up to delight small children, just as dragons and griffins and unicorns came to be known as myths of old, never to truly be believed.

But…throughout time, right up to the modern day, the fae folk have kept an eye on us humans. Some of the old ones still held hope that one day, far into the future, we might begin to see the light, shedding our arrogance to rebuild times past and uniting our forces to begin to heal Mother Earth and put right all those wrongdoings that made our world go awry. And the old ones passed down these prophecies to the younger fae, and so their great hopes for the human race were passed down through the generations, so that sometimes, once in a blue moon, some of them would chance a meeting with some of the more gentle humans, just to keep those strands of hope alive and well.

Sometimes, when a human being is born with their eyes more open than most, when they can see beyond the veil, perceive flashes of a world most choose not to see, the fae will come. Maybe as a flash of light, a wispy shape in the air, a beautiful song on the breeze, sometimes as a fully formed faerie, pixie, imp, dryad, gnome…any kind of magical being whose kin were once allies to our race. When this happens, when one of the fae chooses to show themselves to a human being, they've usually been watching from birth, guiding, assessing, learning to trust us and deciding that hope is not lost.

If you're one of the chosen ones, you should count yourself very lucky and blessed to have been visited by one of the magical ones, for if the fae prophecies are true, it won't be too long now before the scales tip and more humans are ready, willing, humble and sensitive enough to be reunited with the fae kingdoms. And when that happens, balance in our lands will truly be restored.

Beautiful Beginnings: A Tale of Distortion

Long, long ago, back in the times when two-leggeds lived in harmony with the faerie folk, there lived a beautiful princess.

Princess Daeda was the youngest in a long line of fae royalty and, one day, would inherit the role of overseeing the fae queendom from her parents.

From a young age, Princess Daeda had a loyal following; fae from all corners of the known worlds would shower her with gifts and compliments. The pixie folk gifted her with gowns spun from the finest spider silk; the rock people gifted her with beautiful jewels of the most unusual colours; the gnome clan gave the finest, tastiest edible treats to grow from Mother Earth; the elves gifted wondrous tales of magical happenings from the other worlds and the nymphs sang the most beautiful songs to carry her through every emotion. The animal folk and two-leggeds also did their all to shower the princess with affection. The badger clan provided their strongest warriors to guard Princess Daeda and keep her safe; the owl clan kept watch from the skies; the mouse nation paid attention to the closest detail for her and, as she grew, the two-leggeds brought tales of fashions, clothing and strange beauty practices from the tribes across the great seas, carried by travelling tradesmen and bards from other lands.

It's well documented that all fae folk are born with the most magical natural beauty, and Princess Daeda was no exception; with dark hair to rival the blue-black sheen of the raven's wing and sparkling cerulean eyes, clearer than the most crystalline waters, framed by long, luscious lashes. Her full lips were the shade of ripe raspberries and she stood tall, with the most perfect curves developing as she grew. If Princess Daeda was walking the earth today, and in human form, she would most certainly shoot to screen stardom, though our human eyes would undoubtedly be unable to comprehend such shimmering beauty.

Princess Daeda did not want for anything. The riches of the natural world surrounded her, together with more love and support than any one being could ever need.

Alas, it was not enough.

Though happy through her younger years, she began to yearn for the human stories that would be delivered as merchants passed through the faerie woods.

As she grew, she hung on every word and began to reinvent herself, tasking the faefolk to recreate the elaborate costumes she so craved from the two-leggeds' tales.

When she came of age, Princess Daeda began to see a string of suitors – each one braver, more romantic and attractive than the one before. Every time, what began as a magical, seemingly perfect pairing swiftly crumbled to dust as the princess created impossible comparisons with the fantastical stories sung by the human bards.

Every time, the princess would regale her court with stories of her perfect new romance. She would shower her suitors with gifts and all the pleasures available to fae royalty, then expect the impossible in return. Princess Daeda would always believe in the fantasy she created and, each time, she would give a little more of herself, always finding reason to blame her suitor for the demise of their romance. Sometimes they'd be frightened away by the intensity of her demands and overbearing affections, sometimes they were simply unable to reach the impossible heights she demanded, but every time, the relationship would die, together with the fae queendom's hope for a courtship leading to the perfect royal union.

And every time a romance crumbled, Princess Daeda lost a little more of herself.

Those closest to the princess began to recognise that the once-pure soul was being lost to the impossible scenarios weaved by the travelling bards; they knew their princess was searching only for the adventures and romances spun out in the legends, but, in doing so, she was mastering her own ugly destiny. She had everything anyone could ever wish for, yet it would never be enough compared to the fantastical tales she obsessed over.

The royal advisors tried to ban travelling bards from the forest, but the princess would lay down more demands and send her subjects on long, arduous journeys to find more stories from the furthest edges of the earth. Many did not make it back, but this was of little consequence to the princess, who *needed* those stories!

In time, on hearing tales of exotic appearance ideals from far-flung lands, Princess Daeda began to fear her failed relationships stemmed from her not being beautiful enough. Now, as we all know, the fae do not age in the same way as us humans, and it would have been impossible for Princess Daeda to be anything short of stunning to those of us without magical faerie blood running through our veins, but beauty is always in the eye of the beholder. Sometimes, the mirrors we create for ourselves can be full of ugliness and distortion, even when others can only see perfection as their gaze falls upon us.

The fae mage began to be employed by the princess to create magical lotions and potions to change her appearance. Until then, the role of the mage had always been to protect the queendom from harm, care for the sick and advise the royal court, so there was much unease about these new duties. Princess Daeda, though, was determined, and ordered the mage to do as she commanded. Before long, the princess was wearing dark, elaborate stains around her eyes, had changed the shape of her nose, lips and chin. She had ordered the mage to make her taller, thinner, change the fullness of her curves and alter the shimmering hues of her silken hair. Gradually, Princess Daeda became unrecognisable.

When Princess Daeda began to demand animal furs in her costumes, the queendom was in shock. By now, the king and queen had become worn down by her constant demands and were too old and tired to argue; when advisors tried to talk sense into the princess, they were quickly dismissed. In time, to keep peace in the queendom, some of the older animal folk began to offer themselves to her whims.

When the queen and king passed into the Meadows of Change (a joyful, wonderful domain all fae folk return to before being reborn), and Princess Daeda was made queen, she ordered her advisors to create mourning outfits crafted from the softest of badger skins, trimmed with the finest of raven feathers and darkest of wolf claws. Bitter from what she viewed as a lifetime of loss and a dull, grey existence compared to the imagined colours of her stories, Queen Daeda ordered that each of the fae nations offered up hunters to bring her the items required for her wardrobe. When they refused, the queen threatened all kinds of hardships until they relented to safeguard their families.

When the hunters tearfully began to seek out their prey, the animal kingdom began to hide, knowing their lives were in danger, and the hitherto wonderful relationship between earth's furred and feathered clans and the fae folk began to fracture.

After that, Queen Daeda began to read of clothes made from the softest skins, furs carrying the patterns of young fawns, and slippers lined with the silkiest down of the youngest hares. The once beautiful union between all fae clans turned upside down; love turned to hate; support turned to fear; leadership turned to tyranny.

Nobody really knows what happened to Queen Daeda – only that her suitors eventually stopped coming – even when the hunters were sent out to find those deemed suitable and bring them back to the fae court. Queen Daeda gave of herself more and more, but even the most outlandish of gifts and promises could not make the suitors stay with the grotesque queen. Stories of her strange, ill-shaped face and angular physique spread through the faerie queendom and, eventually, found their way back to Queen Daeda through the two-legged bards who took these new 'faerie tales' to the furthest reaches of the known world.

What we do know is that Queen Daeda's advisors eventually stopped advising. The hunters put down their weapons and refused to do more harm. The royal guard refused to harm any more fae on the queen's orders. The entire fae queendom turned their backs on the once-beautiful faerie whose mind had been lost to the destructive fancies of humans.

Unable to face the pain they'd unwittingly wrought on their former allies, the bards began to spin stories of the fae folk into tales of fiction – a final act of apology and aid to help the fae folk remain in hiding forever more.

It's only now that a few courageous fae folk are beginning to trust us humans again and sometimes – just sometimes – a pixie, goblin, elf, faerie or other magical being chooses to show themselves to a human whose heart is open enough to accept them and hold their secrets.

If you're lucky enough to be chosen, dear reader, be sure to hold your tongue and be in gratitude, for our forefathers of oh so long ago were responsible for the worst fate ever to befall the faerie queendom, and their trust in you might just be the most wonderful gift you ever receive.

And one final note – do not befall the same fate as Queen Daeda. Always look for the beauty in your own life, and do not hold yourself in comparison to anyone. You are always, always enough.

The Man and the Frog

Frog was confused. The man, who had been stopping by the pond every morning for as long as he could remember, seemed different today. His shoulders slumped, his feet left furrows instead of clean footprints and his smile was the wrong way up.

Ever since he was a tadpole, Frog had seen the man coming to the edge of the water. He'd greet the sun, the earth and the water spirits and sit in contemplation for a while before leaving to go about his day. Every sunrise, without fail, he would appear, and Frog had grown to appreciate the daily visitor to his home. Usually, the man stood tall and calm and Frog would enjoy watching him go through his daily ritual; he would watch as the man reached high, high, high up towards Grandfather Sun, and as he lay down, belly to the ground, sending love, devotion and thanks to Mother Earth. Sometimes, the man would leave offerings to the tree spirits and, every now and again, he would leave a few tasty morsels for Frog to enjoy with his brothers and sisters. This day, though, the man's arms did not leave his sides. This day, the only skin to connect with the earth was on the soles of the man's feet. This day, he merely glanced up to Father Sky, then down towards Mother Earth, then shook his head and left. Frog hoped the man would be happier after the next sunrise.

The next day, Grandfather Sun rose, in all his shining, fiery glory, as he always does, and Frog waited. He waited patiently. And waited. And waited. The man never came. This became Frog's ritual; he would open his eyes, watch the sun rise, embrace the new day and wait patiently for the man to show up. For almost a moon phase, Frog waited and hoped, but the man did not arrive at the pond.

Just as Frog was beginning to think he should abandon all hope of the man returning, he surfaced from the pond to see the man sitting on the bank. His hair was longer than usual, and his face was thinner, but it was definitely him. Excitedly, Frog swam up to the bank and hopped onto the man's foot, but the man didn't move. Gathering his courage, Frog climbed up to the man's knee, drawn up tightly towards his chest, but still the man didn't acknowledge him. Determined to be seen, Frog sucked in a deep breath and spoke in his loudest voice: 'Ribbit.' The man looked down, but didn't reply.

Frog was confused for a few seconds, then remembered Old Brother Newt talking to him and the other young pond life about the difference in the way humans communicate: 'We newts, frogs, fish, skippers, toads, and even herons,' he'd explained, 'are all different species, yet we can all communicate with one another. Even if Mother Nature created us as natural enemies, we all understand each other when we speak, simply because we communicate from the heart. Mankind lost that ability long ago.'

Squeezing his eyes tight shut, Frog concentrated with all his might and spoke up again, but still the man heard only a croak. Frog kept trying but the man's eyes, red-rimmed and dull, peered down at him with confusion. Frog thought and thought and thought, before clambering up to the man's chest; he placed his hands about where he guessed the man's heart might be and put all his effort into communicating directly with that.

'Hello?' he croaked.

The man gasped.

Looking around and seeing no-one, the man looked down at the frog. 'Did…did you just speak to me?' he asked, with a shaky voice.

Frog smiled and nodded his head. 'Where have you been?' he asked. 'I waited for you and you didn't turn up. Have you been speaking to Grandfather Sun and Mother Earth from somewhere else?'

Frog watched, fascinated, as water began to trail from the man's eyes. 'You're raining!' said Frog. 'How can that be?'

Man shook his head. 'They're tears, Brother Frog. They

sometimes fall when my heart is weeping. More to the point, how can it be that we are able to speak together?'

'Maybe your tears have unblocked your heart enough for you to hear me,' said Frog. 'We communicate differently here. We all speak different languages, but our hearts hear just the same.'

The man nodded and spoke again: 'I have not been coming here because I have been feeling wronged. I felt angry with the Great Shaper and all his allies. I have been coming here for years, speaking my gratitude, making offerings, doing all I can to show my love and devotion, yet I find myself struggling with great hardships.'

Frog didn't understand. 'How is Great Shaper to blame for your life lessons?' he asked. 'Shouldn't this be the time to connect with Grandfather Sun and Mother Earth even more, so you might feel their warmth and support through your struggles?'

Frog felt the man's chest muscles tighten as his dug his fingers deep into the ground. 'Because the Great One shapes everything, including my hardships. How can I leave offerings or share gratitude when everything I hold dear feels threatened?' he asked.

'But Great Shaper only helps bring us the teachings we need,' said Frog. 'What is it you need to learn from these hardships? Perhaps, if you could see that, and be in gratitude for your lessons, the difficulties would dissolve...'

Muscles twitched in the man's jaw and his skin flushed. 'I have been too angry for that,' he snapped.

Frog thought for a moment. 'Old Brother Newt always taught us that anger was a bit of a trickster who hid our real emotions from us. He says anger always sits on top of the real issue, blocking its view and blinding us to the teachings. Anger shields our spirit eyes and binds our hearts with hate...'

The man listened.

'What's beneath your anger?' asked the frog.

The man thought for a moment. 'I'm afraid,' he answered.

Frog patted the man's heart space with his tiny fingers, doing his best to soothe the pain. 'Fear can be crippling too,' he said. 'Sometimes that feels even worse than anger; it can trap us so we feel unable to move. Old Brother Newt says it's like being stuck in a giant spider web and the more we allow it to paralyse us, the thicker the threads binding us become.'

'That's exactly how I feel,' said the man. 'My anger is blocking my gratitude and my fear stops me from moving out of that space.' He looked down at his companion, a single droplet of eye rain sploshing over Frog's head. 'What should I do?' asked the man. 'I'm lost.'

'Move!' said Frog. 'Sometimes the only way to stop being trapped is to decide to not be.'

Frog hopped back down to the man's knee, slid down to his foot, then back onto the ground. 'Watch!' he commanded, before jumping into the pond with a splash.

Frog swam down, through the clear surface of the waters, down deeper, deeper, deeper through the murky depths until he got to the pond bed, where be burrowed down into the mud, before swimming back up to the surface.

Man looked relieved when Frog reappeared, a little muddier than before, but still very much alive. 'Where did you go? I was worried!' said the man.

'Sometimes we need to quest for answers,' said Frog. 'If I get a bit stuck, sometimes I swim right down to the bottom of the pond and burrow down into the mud there... I like to think I'm snuggling into Mother Earth as much as I can, and trust her embrace to bring me the answers I need, as well as comforting me through difficult times. My brothers and sisters sometimes hibernate there and come back feeling refreshed and ready to face the next sunrise, but we never stay there for too long!'

'Why wouldn't you stay there for longer if she's so comforting and safe?' asked the man, feeling frustrated.

Frog shrugged. 'Because we'd drown,' he said.

With that, Frog hopped up onto the bank and stretched out in the daylight. 'Sometimes I do this as well,' he said.

'Do what?' asked the man.

'This!' said Frog. 'I sit with Grandfather Sun, send him my gratitude and feel him connecting back to me. Sometimes I ask him for teachings. He always gives me something wonderful, even if it's just the comfort of his warmth, or the knowledge that he will always show up to share the day with me, so I'm never alone, no matter what.'

'Aah,' said the man, nodding, 'so you can't stay underwater for too long, but you can spend as long as you like on the land.'

'No,' said Frog. 'If I did that, I'd dry out and die.'

Man shook his head. 'So what's the point? What are you trying to tell me?'

Frog hopped back up onto his knee. 'The point, my dear manfriend, is that we always have to move to find the answers we need, and when times are hard, Grandfather Sun always shows up for us, as does Grandmother Moon. Remember that Mother Earth is always supporting us; she cradles us as we sleep, carries our footsteps and catches us when we fall. Always. Without fail.

'When we're feeling caught by anger, or paralysed by fear, it's always best to move. Find stillness if you need to, but find it on *your* terms. Use it to seek the answers you need and don't stay there forever...it's easy to become trapped again if we choose to wallow for too long.'

Man smiled in understanding and offered his palm to Frog as he stood. 'Thank you, Brother,' he said, gently lowering his hand so Frog could hop onto a lily pad, 'I'll see you in the morning.'

The man gave thanks to Grandfather Sun and Mother Earth as he walked away. And his footsteps were lighter.

How Fox Taught the Owls to be Wise

Moonlight flooded the valley with soft, milky hues, casting shadows from the branches of the old oak tree that danced in the gentle breeze.

Fox was out on his usual evening stroll, his belly grumbling at him and nagging him to find something to eat. It had been days now since his last meal. The menfolk in the settlement had become wise to his wily ways; they had created enclosures to protect the hens, and now took turns sitting guard to keep the smaller livestock from his jaws.

The harefolk and rabbit families had heard of Fox's hunger and scuttled beneath the skin of Mother Earth when the other woodland creatures sent word of his approach and even the shrews were finding ways to avoid him these days. This was the way of the wild.

Fox shrugged; perhaps, he thought, he had been enjoying an easy meal for too long... The creatures of the farmstead had provided rich pickings for a long time before his excitement had gotten the better of him. If only he'd stuck to taking one fowl at a time instead of chasing and destroying them all in one wonderful rampage. He felt a happy stupor for a few seconds as he remember the sky filling with feathers and the sounds of chaotic clucking, then shook himself as he realised the consequences of his actions. Hunger. His stomach growled at him again.

Tawny owls called to each other across the valley: 'Tuwit (Brother Fox is prowling),' 'Tuwoo (I know).' Fox barked in frustration. 'How am I ever supposed to find food with you making so much racket?' he demanded. There was silence, then a brief gust of air as the owls landed in front of him.

'Poor Brother Fox,' chuckled Tuwit, 'are you *very* hungry?'
Fox nodded.

'He's very hungry because he's very greedy,' added Tuwoo. 'And noisy.'

'Very stupid too!' said Tuwit.

Fox said nothing.

'Why so quiet?' asked Tuwoo.

Fox whimpered. The owls looked at each other, wondering what was wrong.

'Speak to us, Brother Fox,' said Tuwit, gently reaching out to touch Fox's nose with the tip of his wing. 'We did not realise things were so bad for you.'

Fox said nothing, but sank to the floor with a sigh.

The owls were getting worried now. They circled Fox, every so often nudging him with their heads or gently prodding him with their talons.

'He seems very thin,' worried Tuwit.

'It's far worse than we thought,' agreed Tuwoo, 'he's starving to death!'

The owls huddled, then looked back towards Fox, nodded to each other and flew off. Fox opened one eye and smiled to himself.

Before long, the owls were back. Tuwit dropped a vole at Fox's nose and Tuwoo deposited a field mouse next to it. Fox twitched his nose, but otherwise stayed stock still.

'Brother Fox?' pleaded Tuwit. 'Wake up. We brought food for you!'

Fox let out a small moan, but still didn't move.

'What should we do?' asked Tuwit.

'We will have to feed him,' answered Tuwoo.

Gently, Tuwit fluttered over Fox's head and used his talons to gently grasp either side of his muzzle and pull open his mouth. Tuwoo picked up the vole and dropped it into Fox's mouth.

The owls stood back. Fox did nothing.

'It's in your mouth, Brother Fox,' said Tuwit.

'You need to eat,' added Tuwoo.

Ever so slowly, making his efforts look as weak and feeble as he could, Fox chewed the vole and swallowed it down.

'Is that better?' asked Tuwit.

Fox made a show of trying to nod his thanks, but seemed too weak to lift his head.

'He needs more,' said Tuwoo. 'Let's feed him the mouse you found.'

The owls repeated the exercise with the field mouse, but still Fox seemed weak. They exchanged a look, then flew off to find more food.

By the time Grandfather Sun was beginning to rise, the owls had fed Fox a feast of woodland fare, but still they were concerned.

'Brother Fox,' asked Tuwit, peering closely, 'can you stand? You shouldn't stay out in daylight when the menfolk are hunting you.'

Fox tried to stand, but pretended to have shaky legs and wobbled back to the ground. 'I'm not sure I can move,' he said quietly. 'Thank you for all your help, but I'm afraid I am done for. Leave me here and go off to the safety of your treetops.'

Tuwit and Tuwoo exchanged worried glances, then swooped one wing each beneath Fox's chest and half carried, half dragged him back to his den. Once Fox was safely inside, the owls told him to stay put and promised to bring food the next night.

For almost a whole moon phase, Fox lazed in the luxury of his den, growing fuller and fatter and feigning weakness every night while the owls hunted for him and brought food to his bedside. 'Now who's stupid?' Fox grinned to himself.

One night, when Fox decided he'd had enough of rodents and berries, he sauntered out of his den and made his way towards the village. It had been so long since his chicken rampage that the menfolk had stopped worrying about him – nobody stood guard and the hens were roaming free once more. Holding himself in check, he quickly and quietly stole just one hen, then carried it off to the woodlands to enjoy a sumptuous supper.

As he made his way to his den, Fox stopped by the owl tree and called up to his unwitting servants: 'Hey Tuwit, Tuwoo, I heard you were hungry.' He laughed, dropping his leftovers at the base of trunk.

Tuwit and Tuwoo had been so long caring for Fox that they hadn't been eating enough for themselves. Skinny and starving, they dropped down and ate everything they found there. Pretty soon they began to cough and spat out pellets of nothing, but bone and feather.

'How could you?' shrieked Tuwit. 'We fed you for days and you bring us dry remains.'

'Because I'm greedy and stupid – you said so yourself,' laughed Fox. 'Maybe you will be wiser in future!'

With that, Fox went back to his den, full of food and mirth.

To this day, foxes are still known to be the most cunning creatures in the countryside, and owls have learned to be the wisest!

The Fearie

What is it that you fear, child? What is it that grips you so and holds you back? What is it that stops you from living your dreams?

We all have something; some horrid little nightmare thought that grows arms and fingers and legs and claws and holds onto our heart with steadfast determination. He pinches and squeezes and flexes his talons, and he always knows precisely how tightly to apply his grip, so we might still see our hopes, yet feel our souls sink as we begin to believe they are out of reach.

He is not real, you know, this fear-giving imp. He only lives because we allow him to. We are his host – we shelter him with our bodies, feed him with our negativity, water him with our dread. We call him The Fearie, and he resides in every one of us.

Do not be deceived, little one, for The Fearie does not haunt you alone. The strongest warrior, the wisest elder, the kindest mother, the tiniest bairn, even the most ferocious of hounds all take visitation from The Fearie, and the tales he spins are different for every one of us. He is clever, The Fearie; he always knows exactly what to whisper into our hearts to allow the dread to rise up, yet he is not undefeatable.

Understand that at the very beginnings of your life, The Fearie had an honourable task in keeping you safe... It was The Fearie who stopped you putting your hands into the beautiful flames, The Fearie who stopped you believing you could safely fly from the highest branches, The Fearie who stopped you from leaping into deep waters before your body had learned to float and swim. It was only as you grew older that The Fearie's mission became distorted. As you grew to understand life's dangers and began to develop the common sense to keep you from harm, The Fearie's job became smaller, so he had to find another way. And you gave him new tasks, my child... We all did!

As we grew, we allowed The Fearie to take hold of all those tiny insecurities and nurture them into fears; new experiences became terrifying bridges to cross, big tasks became scary and seemed insurmountable, cruel and throwaway remarks from other people became daggers piercing our confidence and convincing us we simply weren't good enough. All this and more, dear one, has been the work of The Fearie.

I told you before that The Fearie could be beaten, and I was telling no lie, yet the defeat of The Fearie can first make him stronger and only the bravest of hearts may succeed in their quest. You see, child, in order to beat The Fearie, we must recognise him, name him and choose to disbelieve the terror spells he weaves in order to melt away his powers.

In order to defeat The Fearie, you must question every fear that begins to rise up inside of you; you must examine and scrutinise to check for truths and, sooner or later, a pattern will begin to emerge. You will see that the thoughts that bred fear in your belly were nothing but thoughts...and thoughts can be dismissed by choice. You will see that the negative self beliefs you thought true have been false all along. You will realise that the new situations unfolding may be wonderful and full of opportunities but that, somewhere along the path, The Fearie created confusion between excitement and fear, and that you have the absolute ability to choose either emotion.

Take small steps along this road to control, little one. Where you believe 'everyone' dislikes you, find one person who loves you with all their heart; do you see? That belief simply is not true, and once you've identified that tiny hole in your theory, you can find more and more people who actually like you and explode that entire myth. Where you fear something is too scary to even comprehend, break down your fears into little pieces until they no longer make sense; if you are afraid of spiders, try to remember when you first learned that fear, then work out what, exactly, you believe you are afraid of... Is it the swift movement?

Would they still be scary if they moved at a snail's pace? Is it all the legs? Who else do you know with legs? Are they scary? What would a spider have to do to make friends with you? What if they started delivering your favourite treats, or spinning lovely words for you to wake up to in the morning? Try learning everything you can about them; what are their skills? How many sorts are there? Which ones have you seen? How long does it take them to spin a web? Are spiders really so terrifying? One day, when you're brave enough, you'll be able to gently scoop up one of the Spider Clan and marvel at their beauty and ingenuity...and then, my dear, The Fearie's work will be undone.

What if you fear you are not good at anything? This is just another of The Fearie's tricks. What *are* you good at? Trust me here – there will be many things. Are you good at breathing? What about walking? Can you do that? Do you know how to bathe yourself? Do you know how to eat? How to drink? There must be a million and one things you are good at; I won't know all of them, but, if you take the time to make a list of *everything* you can do, The Fearie's game will soon be over.

Remember, The Fearie can only control us if we allow just that. You are now equipped with a very special weapon, for you know how to defeat him, and you know how to help others do the same. Perhaps, when you have mastered defeat of The Fearie enough, you will be able to help other people conquer their fears as well...and that, dear one, is the mark of a very brave warrior indeed.

The Listening Tree

There is a tree that stands tall and proud in the forest. Its branches reach almost as far as it is tall, falling into a blissful green canopy. Grandfather Sun shines his warming light between the leaves and the rain spirits sometimes rest upon them, before drip, drip dropping down to moisten the ground below. This is the Listening Tree. It has been there far longer than any other tree in the forest; its roots reach deep, deep down into Mother Earth and its highest limbs reach out to join Father Sky.

For as long as any of us can remember, people have visited the Listening Tree; it has long been a place of solace and healing for those with heavy hearts and sorry stories to share. And the tree listens. It always listens. People reach out and place their palms against its gnarly skin, or sit and rest their backs against its welcoming trunk. Sometimes people weep. Sometimes they just talk, for minutes or hours. Sometimes people leave offerings at its base, or tie prayers into its branches. Always, people leave less burdened, standing taller and with a hint of promise in their eyes.

The Listening Tree must be thousands of years old...older, perhaps, than you or I might be able to comprehend. What stories it must have seen unfold. What beauty, magic and wisdom it must have gathered. It stands there, tall and proud and silent, never sharing secrets, only ever listening, holding and providing support for all who need it.

We could all learn so much from its purity and strength. The Listening Tree asks for nothing, yet stands for so much.

Perhaps there is a listening tree in woodlands near you. Perhaps, dear one, there exists a tree just for you – a place for support, sharing, even confessions. When people feel they can speak to nobody else, when the secrets are too great or the sorrow too deep, the Listening Tree I sing of is always ready to hear, always ready to absorb sadness, anger, frustration, guilt, grief and every other emotion known to man; and when it has heard our words, it transmutes that energy into something pure and good to send deep down into Mother Earth, goodness seeping through its roots back to the core.

When you find your tree, child – and I know there will be one close to you somewhere – remember to gift it with happiness too; allow your tree to take your problems and woes, but remember to share joy and laughter also. When you can feel it taking your sadness, perhaps give thanks with a song, or your favourite humorous tale, a dance, a hug, some love. For if the tree is listening, it seems only right to provide lightness to balance the shadows of our hearts.

Grumblethwick's Bad Day

Grumblethwick was having a bad day. He didn't entirely know why. Nothing had particularly gone wrong. Nothing had particularly changed. Nobody had upset or angered him. Today though, his heart (for he did have a heart, though it might not be the same as yours or mine) felt heavy.

Awkwardly, he lumbered about his home, secreted deep beneath the roots of the mighty oak. He could tell by the smell of the air that Grandfather Sun was shining brightly this day, warming away the wetness of the thunder beings and storm sylphs that had visited a few nights before, yet even this did not lighten his mood.

With a sigh, Grumblethwick slumped to the earthen floor, his back resting against the side of a tree root. He did not even notice when Brother Badger poked his nose into the room; Grumblethwick was far too taken up with his own miserable musings to take note of his visitor until Brother Badger squeezed all the way in and sat in front of him.

Grumblethwick raised a brow, but said nothing.

'What's the matter with you?' asked Brother Badger, dropping a worm that had been balancing on his snout at Grumblethwick's feet.

'Not hungry,' Grumblethwick replied. Badger shrugged and swallowed the worm himself.

'We can feel your mood all over the woods,' said Badger. 'Well, at least as far out as the pine forest. What's going on?'

Grumblethwick scuffed one gnarly foot against the ground, but said nothing.

Badger waited. He was good at waiting. He'd wait here all day if he needed to.

Grumblethwick still said nothing.

Badger nudged Grumblethwick's foot with his paw and

cleared his throat. Perhaps he wasn't so patient after all.

'The gnomes say you're depressed,' Badger prodded, 'and if *they're* noticing a dour mood, it *has* to be bad. You know how little regard they pay to what's going on around them usually. I'd expect a giant forest fire before anything shook them, or maybe the river bursting its banks and beginning to flood the dell.'

Grumblethwick rested his knotted chin on his hand, but still said nothing.

'Come on,' said Badger, 'this isn't like you. Nobody expects a tree troll to be the life and soul of the forest floor, but *some* life signs would be useful...'

'I just don't feel like doing much,' said Grumblethwick. 'I woke up feeling this way, and I don't know why.'

Badger stroked his hairy chin and pondered for a moment. 'Have the dreamweavers been bothering you?' he asked.

'No. Haven't remembered my night journeys for weeks,' said Grumblethwick.

'Are you lonely then?' asked Badger. 'Because there's a moss maiden down by the stream and I'm sure her magicks jump up a notch when you're close by.'

Grumblethwick shook his head. 'I know you're trying to help, Brother Badger, but I fear I may be beyond saving today.' He sniffed and a single droplet of tree resin fell from his eye and trickled down his cheek.

Badger didn't quite know what to do next. He thought about inviting Grumblethwick down to the sycamore grove, where it was race season for the spinning seeds, who always grew competitive over who could reach the ground first, then he thought about taking him across to the stream, where the water nymphs were frolicking and making foam baths between the stones, but Grumblethwick didn't seem willing to move.

'*That's it!*' thought Badger, '*I need to get him to move. The happiest creatures in the forest are the faeries, and they're always zipping about all over the place. Maybe that's why they're so happy!*'

Badger stood up, turned around and shook his tail, sending a spray of fine soil all over Grumblethwick.

Spluttering, Grumblethwick jumped up and brushed himself down. 'What did you do that for?!' he demanded.

'I did that,' said Badger, 'because I think you're sitting in a sad spot and I needed a way to get you up! Come on...' With that, Badger grabbed Grumblethwick's twiggy fingers between his claws and began to drag him up through the door between the tree roots.

'But I don't want to go,' complained Grumblethwick.

Badger ignored him and kept going, squashing himself through the doorway and pulling the depressed tree troll behind him. Badger gave such a yank when he reached the great outdoors that Grumblethwick flew up through the entrance and landed in a heap on the floor. Slowly, Grumblethwick opened his eyes and looked up, only to see all the creatures of the forest surrounding him – animals, birds, creepers and crawlers, as well as many different varieties of fae.

'What are you all looking at?' he asked, glumly.

Sister Deer took a tentative step forwards and looked softly at Grumblethwick. 'We all felt your sadness,' she said gently. 'You may have been hiding out under the oak tree, but we are all connected, and your sadness sent ripples through the forest. We were worried about you.'

Grumblethwick looked up at her and caught another droplet of sap with his fingertip before it rolled down his face. 'I am sorry, Sister Deer,' he said, 'I did not know my mood would upset anyone else.'

One of the gnomefolk stepped forward next. 'People think we're too busy going on with our own business to notice what's going on around us, Grumblethwick, but when one heart is heavy, we feel our own become a little weightier too. Something about the energy around here changes...it's like your little storm cloud casts a shadow over everyone else.'

Grumblethwick stood and looked at all the beings around him. None of them seemed angry with him, even though his bad mood seemed to have infected the forest. Right then, he realised how much he was loved and cared for, and he knew he had to find a way to climb out of his doldrums.

'I don't want to feel like this,' he said, addressing the crowd gathered before him. 'I just don't know how to shake it off. It's not as if anything happened to cause it… I just woke up feeling glum.'

Brother Woodpecker flew down and settled in front of him. 'When I'm feeling a bit down, I just peck at some wood and it always makes me feel better,' he said. Grumblethwick just managed to dodge out of the way as Woodpecker's sharp bill headed for his knee.

'I like to gnaw on things,' said Brother Beaver, making a beeline for Grumblethwick's ankle. Again, the tree troll just managed to move out of the way in time.

'We like to burrow!' said a trio of young rabbits, diving for the earth around Grumblethwick's feet and forcing him to hop to one side.

'I swoop around and find twigs for our nest,' said the red kite. Grumblethwick jumped forward, just as the talons aimed for his head.

'We like to make hills!' said the ant colony, and Grumblethwick soon skipped to another spot as the earth beneath his feet began to move.

Grumblethwick felt something land on his head and looked up, only to start dancing about to avoid more missiles being aimed at him from above. 'We like to throw acorns at people,' giggled the squirrel clan from high in the treetops.

'Why you mischief makers!' laughed Grumblethwick, unable to hold onto his sadness as the other forest creatures began to laugh at the antics of everyone trying to cheer up the tree troll, and how their actions had forced Grumblethwick to dance around the floor.

'How are you feeling now, Grumblethwick?' asked one of the forest faeries, fluttering around in the air before him. 'Are you any happier?'

Grumblethwick smiled: 'As a matter of fact, I feel wonderful,' he said, dancing a little jig around the base of the tree. 'Thank you all for making me feel so happy.'

'You're welcome,' said the faerie. 'We don't always know why we feel glum, but there's always a way to find your smile...sometimes, you just need to dance around for a while and your smile will find *you*.'

Grinning from ear to ear, Grumblethwick nodded. 'I suppose that's why you faerie folk are always so cheery,' he said. 'It's because you never stay still.'

'Something like that,' the faerie replied, 'and remembering how much we're loved helps too.'

Brother Badger smiled knowingly. He'd been right all along...movement *does* help to shake a bad mood, and it doesn't only work for faeries!

The Girl Who Lived in the Stone House

The walls of the stone house vibrated with every beat of her heart. Nobody else would have noticed, but the girl did. The walls moved in closer every day. They protected her, kept her safe, but every day they came closer. Closer. Closer. Some days, it felt difficult to breathe. Some days, the walls felt so close that the girl could almost feel their coldness on her skin. Some days she was afraid to stretch too far in case the tips of her fingers scraped the harshness of the stones. It was getting tight. Too tight. But it was keeping her safe.

Nobody knew about the girl in the stone house. Nobody knew she was there. Nobody saw her, trapped inside. Nobody understood what was happening to her. Nobody could help.

Only she could help herself. And only then if she chose to.

But it was safe inside her house of stone. Nobody could touch her there. The only trouble was, she couldn't touch anybody either.

If she thought, really thought back hard, the girl could remember laying down the very first stone of the first wall. The clay was made from sadness, held together with tears. She could remember making the stone from her emotions, so many years ago, after she'd sat holding her grandfather's hand as he left his body behind and his soul went exploring in the next place. She didn't like to say he'd died, because he'd always live on in her heart, and the soul doesn't really die anyway – it just goes off to live somewhere else. She'd tried to be happy for him, knowing he'd been able to leave his worn-out old body behind, but she still felt sad about not being able to sit with him at the fireside any more, about not being able to hear his gravelly voice telling her stories of old, or weaving wonderful teachings about the stars and the trees and all the creatures of this world and the other worlds. He was wise, her grandfather and, even though she knew his aches and pains were growing at a faster rate than his years, she had desperately wanted him to stay – there was never enough time. When he finally left his body, she'd spilled more tears than she had ever believed she could and, when the tears became overwhelming, she willed them to dry up. And that's when the first stone was born. She boxed up her sadness and turned it into the first brick of her stone house…and a little piece of her left with it.

Since then, the girl had created many more stones and the walls had built up thick and high all around her until her house had become a prison. There was a stone in the wall for her little brother, who was born into the world without his breath, and there were stones for her parents who had been asking for a bairn for so long. There was a stone for the argument she'd had with her best friend, just before her family had left the settlement, there was a stone for her faithful hound who had never returned from the hunt and there was a stone for the grandmother she'd never met, but had lived so vividly through her grandfather's stories. There was a stone for the farmer whose crops had failed, there was a stone for the worry of the villagers who wondered how they might survive the colder months without the wheat and corn, there was a stone for the time she fell down and hurt her knee and there was a stone for that look in her mother's eyes when the bread she was meant to be watching had been ruined by the heat. For every upset in the girl's life, there was a stone, and the stone walls now reached higher and further than she could see.

By the time the girl reached her teenage years, she was untouchable – or, at least, that's what people thought. She had no friends, because the invisible stones kept them out, and she sometimes heard grownups in the village whispering about her being strange or withdrawn. Her parents cared for her – she was sure of that – although she didn't really understand what that meant. All those stones, borne out of pain and fear and tears, had formed a barrier around her heart. She hadn't thought about it much at the time – she'd just wanted the pain to stop and she desperately wanted to avoid feeling anything like that in the future. Her house – prison – of stone was highly effective, but what she hadn't considered was that she couldn't pick and choose the feelings she wanted to keep or discard; the walls kept *everything* out until she couldn't really feel much from the outside world at all.

These prisons of our own making also carry other problems...when those walls are too close, we become brittle and removed, and we can become callous with our own words and thoughts, because the feelings we do have stay trapped inside, so our anger and frustrations stay with us in our self-made cell. We might not feel the hurt from the outside world as much, but the feelings that begin inside us have no way to disperse.

That's what happened to the girl. She didn't realise how distant she'd become and she didn't know how many of the wonders of life she was shutting out. Until the day it happened. The day the girl did something so courageous, so incredible that it would change her life forever. It might even change your life too, little one, for stories all carry magical messages and secret teachings and, if the Great Shaper has dropped this story onto your path, it will have been no accident!

Sometimes, when the girl was feeling especially uncomfortable with all the hustle and bustle of the village, she would take herself off to the woodlands...it was right on the edge of the settlement and quite safe. She would sit in solitude, running thoughts through her head and wondering what all the fuss was about. People, she decided, were stupid to expend so much energy on pointless emotions – just thinking about it made her angry. She didn't feel particularly strange and she didn't understand why more people wouldn't want to keep themselves to themselves more than they did – fewer people would get hurt that way and all those tears and upset – as well as merriment and frivolity – felt like such a waste of time.

On the day it happened, the girl was sitting in her usual woodland clearing. Days before, a great storm had come and some of the weaker trees had been felled by the powerful winds. There was much drama in the village, with people making repairs to lodges, clearing away debris and, of course, many people shedding tears over lost things and ruined crops. She remembered the last time the people had worried over the loss of grain and berated herself for the tears she'd wasted back then. What did crying solve? Nothing. The girl felt nothing but irritation this time and she'd said as much to the farmer's wife, who only cried more on hearing her words; one of the farmhands had overheard and came towards her red-faced and shouting, and that's when she'd decided to go to the woodlands instead. There was no point in staying with the villagers – nobody seemed to want her help and they were so quick to anger if she tried to help by sharing her wisdom.

So, there she sat, wringing her hands and wondering about her place in the world. And that was when it happened.

A little way ahead, the girl noticed movement in the under-growth; she listened and listened, but could not work out what was causing the sound. Slowly, she stood up and began to move towards the place where the tree had fallen. At first, the girl could not see anything but then, as she crouched close to the ground and peered between the leaves and branches, she saw the most beautiful, deep brown eye staring back at her. Framed by the darkest lashes, the eye belonged to a young doe; gently, the girl moved her hand towards the animal's face, clearing away some of the branches and brushing away flies who were being far too intrusive far too soon. The deer blinked and let out a shallow breath, and it dawned on the girl that this beautiful creature may not have many left to give. Catching the animal's gaze, the girl felt a strange twisting in her heart...an emotion she had not felt for many years; she pondered it for a second before hearing her grandfather's gravelly words in her head: 'All life is precious, child, and every living being is connected – no one soul is more, or less, important than the next. We each have our part to play in the great web of life.' Her breath caught in her chest and long-lost emotions began to rise up and the first of the stone blocks the girl had created so many years ago began to crumble away.

Wiping away a stray tear from her face, the girl stood and followed the line of the tree, only to see that it had trapped the doe as it had crashed to the ground; the trunk of the tree lay dangerously across the gentle creature's hind quarters, holding her solidly to the ground. The girl spoke in hushed tones and stroked the deer's face, whispering reassurances as she promised to do all she could to help. Standing, she picked her way through the debris until she reached the foot of the fallen tree. She tried to lift it away, but had not enough strength in her arms. Thinking hard, she tried to find a solution and came up with nothing.

'If only grandfather was still here,' she thought, 'he was the wisest of men in the village...he would know what to do.'

Memories of the girl's grandfather began to swim to the surface of her mind and she felt a strange tingling sensation as more and more of the stones she'd created began to dissolve; she thought of her dear, lost hound and found herself smiling as more tears came, 'like a rainbow through a rainstorm,' she realised. Blinking through her tears, the girl made her way back to the deer's face, leaning in close and allowing the tears to fall.

'Tell me what to do,' she choked. 'You are too precious and too beautiful to end here like this.'

She didn't recognise the voice at first – it carried a warmth that flooded her heart with emotions so long held back, and felt to her as if it carried the combined wisdom and knowing of all the stars in the skies. 'You must choose now, child,' said the voice. 'Opening a heart closed for so long is the bravest of things...there is so much for you to learn, so much for you to do. Open your heart, dear one...choose to feel again – there is enough joy to balance sadness, enough love to balance fear, there is enough of everything you will ever need, if only you allow yourself to feel it.'

At first, the girl wondered if it was the spirit of the doe talking to her, and then she felt a strand of remembering begin to touch her heart – this was the voice of her grandmother, a woman she had never met, yet had been made real through her grandfather's storyweaving.

The girl looked down at the doe, pulling a strand of love, buried deep in her heart and sending it straight to the beautiful wild animal. 'I will help you,' she promised. 'I will be brave. I will trust my grandmother's words and do what I can.' Softly, she dropped a small kiss on the deer's cheek and stood up.

Moving back towards the base of the tree, the girl tried again to move the weighty branches. Tears of frustration began to fall and she wondered how on earth she would complete this impossible task.

'It is time, dear child,' came her grandmother's voice once more, and right there and then, she knew what she must do. Facing the sun, the girl focussed on her heart space and sent a cord of golden light up to the skies. As she felt Grandfather Sun return her warmth, the girl forced herself to remember every time she'd ever been hurt in her entire life – she remembered her grandfather's passing and the loss of her beloved hound, she remembered her parents' grief when her baby brother had been born still; she thought about the plight of the village when the crops failed, and she even made herself focus on the whispers of the villagers who called her strange and withdrawn. As she thought on each of these times, she allowed her tears to fall once more but, as wetness streaked her young face, she reached not only for the sadness, but for the love she had once held so dear. Even when it came to the words of the villagers, she sought not to feel unkindness, but to feel their concern for the young girl who had once felt too overwhelmed to cope with all the world had to offer. As she thought of all the memories she'd tried to box away, she saw the little bricks she'd created in her mind's eye and willed them to dissolve. Finally, as the last of the girl's invisible walls came tumbling down, she opened her heart fully, as only the bravest of warriors are able.

As the girl's heart opened, she felt all the energies of the universe around her as golden light surrounded her heart. She felt able to tap into all the strands of strength and love from the natural world and she willed them into her heart, through her arms and down to her hands. Finally, with her heart filled with love and possibility, she reached for the base of the tree again and effortlessly moved it away from the doe.

Eyes wide and heart full, the girl hurriedly returned to gaze into the doe's beautiful, deep brown eyes. 'Stay here,' she said. 'Do not try to move... I will fetch my father who will be able to help you.'

The eyes of the village turned to the girl as she ran into the settlement, tears streaming and voice full of joy. Her father, having not seen his precious child so full of life in more seasons than he could remember, was only too pleased to go with her and save this deer that had such a miraculous effect on her. Neither of them quite understood what had happened when they reached the clearing, only to find the tree still perfectly rooted into Mother Earth and no doe anywhere to be seen.

From that day on, the girl determined to keep her heart open and to send love to all who needed it, doing her very best to prevent others from creating stones to block their hearts. She became known as the Deer Girl, and villagers spoke of her shining eyes and sunshine heart, in place of the withdrawn, strange girl she once was.

It was three summers later when the new family was accepted into the settlement – two parents with one child about the same age as the girl. Villagers always said the fates had intervened to join the two souls together, and the girl had known a new level of love immediately – as soon as she had gazed into the newcomer's beautiful, deep brown eyes, framed by the darkest lashes.

The Standing People

Never be too proud to share your sorrows with the trees.
For trees are the Standing People,
steeped with knowledge and deeply rooted.

The Standing People will not judge,
for they have witnessed far worse
and are wise enough to see the light in your heart.

The Standing People's roots reach deep into Mother Earth;
who better to hear your woes and send your problems
back to the earth to be absorbed and transformed into light?

Just as your woes will go back to the earth,
your light will be amplified by sunlight, through the tree's
limbs.

Always talk to the trees.

Chapter 3

Channelling Your Own Stories

If you want to have a go at channelling some stories of your own, there are lots of methods you can try, depending on your levels of experience. Right back at the beginning of this book, I spoke about the importance of beginning to exercise our 'bardic muscles' and one of the ways to start doing this is to re-weave some of your favourite stories from childhood. Try not to go back and re-read them – just retell whatever you can remember and put your own spin on it. Or, if there are particular teachings you want to deliver with your tales, think about how you might be able to work these into stories you're already familiar with. You might want to write the stories down, speak them into a voice recorder or speak them aloud to friends, family, perhaps even larger audiences if your confidence allows.

Once you're used to storytelling, you might want to start to seek some of your own, asking spirit for guidance and, perhaps, to share some long-lost stories of old with you. As with any energy or spirit work, it's a good idea to make sure your house is in order. By this, of course, I mean your energy body. Depending on which area of energy work you're used to, you might want to start with some grounding and protection; spend a little time in meditation, check your chakras are all nicely aligned and that your aura is smooth and intact, and check that you are properly connected and rooted safely to Mother Earth – there are plenty of meditation soundtracks available that will help you do this if need be.

When you feel ready to go, one of the easiest ways is to try sourcing a story through meditation. If you're doing this at home, check your phones are switched off, do your best to make sure nobody will be knocking at your door or disturbing you for a while, and make yourself as comfortable as possible. You might choose to burn some incense or light a candle; with these methods, you can concentrate on the smoke/vapours from the incense, or gaze at the candle flame, as part of your meditation, though some people prefer to simply close their eyes and focus on their breathing to get into a meditative state. Try to clear your mind, except for holding onto your intention – to be gifted with a teaching story – and wait for the magic to happen.

I cannot stress strongly enough that there is no right or wrong way to do this. So many people see meditation as some unattainable holy grail, accessible only by a special few who are able to reach 'nothingness' easily. For me, this could not be further from the truth. While it's true that some people find it easier to switch off than others, you absolutely do not need to be aiming for a perfect sense of peace straight away. It's as simple as carving out some quiet time, making your surroundings as comfortable and peaceful as possible, and setting your intention to leave the stresses and strains of the day behind. Find that quiet, peaceful state and simply try asking to be gifted with a story. If you've never tried meditation before, you might want to use a meditation CD or download; I'd go for one without spoken word, so you can hold to your intention instead of being guided along another path for another time. Again, go for whichever one feels right for you, whether drums, chimes, white noise, ambient music, nature sounds or anything else out there – anything that helps you switch off and relax will do just fine. It may be that you'll need to try several before you find one that works for you, or you might find that different sound bases bring about different depths of meditation.

Although I thank the 'ancestors' for my stories, I don't see any reason why you shouldn't ask whichever beings you work with most to come forward with your story – be that angels, the universe, animal guides, or dear departed Auntie Ethel. Simply put, your comfort zone will probably be different according to the energies you're most used to working with. Someone who works with angel cards will probably feel more comfortable working with different spirits to someone who practices spiritualism, or animism, or anything else. Start with the way of working you're most familiar with and move on from there.

Try not to get too hung up on the way the stories are presented to you. I have always been predominantly visual in terms of senses, but remember there's no right or wrong here – you might at first get a few words, a few random images, some sounds or sensations or you might be lucky enough to be gifted with a full story being played out in glorious Technicolor straight away. Whatever happens, set yourself a time limit for your meditations, perhaps consider setting a gentle alarm to alert you and help you to come back to the present, and be sure to write everything down straight away. Don't be dissuaded if you don't succeed on your first attempt – just keep setting your intention, finding time and space to meditate and asking for a story. It might come in lots of tiny pieces, it might come all at once, just keep trying and keep heart.

Another way is to venture out into the great outdoors. Find a space, out in nature and, when you're ready, find a place to sit and tune in. When I was channelling the stories for this book, I found some of the trees to be wonderfully gentle protectors and more than happy to share some stories with me. Just take a few moments to think about all our more mature trees must have witnessed over the years – they have stood by for more years than many of us could even imagine and must hold so much wisdom. I like to take an offering if I'm working out in nature – perhaps a pinch of tobacco, a little milk, a few strands of my hair, whatever feels appropriate – occasionally, I've even gifted a small crystal, sometimes burying it just beneath the surface soil near the trunk. Tune in to the tree and, perhaps, ask if you might lean against it and feel its embrace. When you feel the time is right, sink back against the tree, give thanks and ask to be gifted with a story. As before, don't put too much pressure on yourself – or Spirit – to gift you with an entire story straight away; just trust to be patient. Another tip: so long as you're in a safe place, don't worry if you happen to fall asleep against the tree...remember stories can come in the dreamtime too, and one of the most beautiful encounters I had with a tree spirit came as I slept against its trunk.

Those of you who are used to trance work or shamanic journeying can, of course, use these methods. Journey to your most trusted guides and ask them to gift you with a story, or ask them to introduce you to an ancestor spirit who might be willing to pass down a story for you to share with the world. If you're used to using these methods, you might want to try working with the land spirits to source stories too, as well as some of the more ancient energies we might find out in nature; I've found old ones such as rocks and trees have fascinating stories to share. In every case, remember to check if you're allowed to pass on the story and remember to always give thanks for all you're gifted with.

On every occasion, write down everything you're given as soon as you can – it's very easy for our minds to get in the way and start either deleting details or adding in content to fill the gaps, so noting everything down straight away will result in the purest retelling.

Chapter 4

Stories from Others

Through my workshops and teachings, I have shared these story-weaving exercises with many people over the past few years. Some have been able to channel beautiful stories of their own, and I'm sharing a selection here – with the authors' permission – to show how different they can all be, and – of course – that these stories are available to all with pure and open hearts and good intent who quest for them.

Some come in the form of stories, some as poetry and some as an almost historical re-telling. Remember, there really is no right or wrong – notice the different styles here and the different teachings that come through for you.

I look forward to reading many channelled stories to come, from all corners of the globe, and I look forward to reading some of the stories *you* uncover after reading this book. If you'd like to share your work with me, do look me up and drop me a line!

The Goose Girl

By Jackie Flynn

Each year the geese came. Flying across the skies in enormous v shapes. The people of the flat lands always knew when the geese were coming. They could feel them, sense them, hear them deep within their hearts, long before their eyes had sight of them.

The children would run outside and wait. Looking up into the massive expanse of sky. Shielding their eyes from the sun with their hands. Each child wanted to be the first to catch sight of the geese as they came into view on the horizon. The older children ran to a higher vantage point, jostling with each other, pushing the smaller children out of the way.

The sounds came first. The haunting cries filling the skies and the ears of the people with their songs, their tales of where they had been. Oh, the stories they told to those who could hear.

The older people of the tribe would sit and watch and wait. They too felt the return of the geese in their hearts. The feeling brought a melancholy, a knowing of time passing, a remembering of their own childhoods and of those who were no longer with them in this life. The returning geese signalled the turning of the year. A time of deep winter, aching cold, death and birth.

The people lived by the seasons. They knew the signs of the changes as they knew the lines on their lovers' faces and the creases in the tiny hands of their newborn babies. They knew the meaning of a bird call, the way the fish swam in the river. They knew, deep within their bones, the meanings in the mists that swirled across the fens, engulfing all in a cloak of invisibility.

The people took their living from this land and from these rivers. The women planted by the turning of the moon. It was a hard, but good, life.

The people lived a peaceful life and each life was precious.

Lovers made their sounds in the still of the night, their gasps whispering across the settlement, causing the children to stifle laughter and bring smiles to the faces of the old ones who knew after the turning of nine moons a woman would enter the birthing hut. Her cries and moans being heard by all as she struggled to bring a new life to the tribe.

The small baby girl was born as the first geese flew overhead. Their songs drowning out the cries of the woman who knew her baby had come too soon. The longed for first child. The mother wept silent tears as she held her newborn daughter to her breast. She knew, deep inside, that this child would not live to see her first sunset.

As she sat and rocked her baby she began to sing. At first a low tuneless hum. Then gradually louder yet still softly her voice could be heard by all as she sang the wordless song the women would sing to all who were returning home to the lands of the ancestors, the ones who had walked these lands before, whose bones and blood are still in the land for all to walk on.

The geese flying high above the woman and her child heard the song and, one by one, slowed their flight as they looked down on the sight of the mother and child. Her calling home song rose to meet the song of the geese and for a while, time stood still, and to those who watched and to those who could see, the geese appeared motionless in the skies and a circle of ancestors formed around the woman and child. The ancestors of the child and her mother, and of the people of this land formed circles within circles holding the child and her mother safe. Her song was now suspended in the cold evening air as the sun made its journey below the far horizon.

The mother stopped her singing and gazed up into the darkening skies to see the geese moving away into the distance. Their still mournful song calling to her. Yet seemingly different somehow.

She then looked down into the face of her newborn child and

pulled her close to her. Her tears fell onto the closed eyes of her baby and she was certain she would hold her child until the time came to pass her into the safe arms of the ancestors, who by now had surrounded the mother and child in a loving embrace.

The mother then slept. Still sitting. Still holding her now cold child.

The songs of the geese grew more and more faint until a mist of silence fell across the land.

Morning came. The sun rose from its sleep. As did the mother. For a moment she was still in the dream. A dream where she could still hear the songs of the geese. As she woke further she shifted slightly and felt the weight of her child in her arms. At that moment the events of the past day and night came flooding back into her mind. It was then that she felt a movement. She looked down and through her wet eyelashes she could see two brilliant blue eyes staring back at her. Eyes that pierced deep into her soul with an ancient knowing.

A hungry wail escaped from the child's mouth as she sought out the milk that was now pouring from the mother's breast.

As the mother moved to allow her daughter to feed, she noticed, hidden deep within the folds of the cloth she had wrapped her child in, a single white goose feather.

The little girl thrived and grew, living for many years amongst her people. She was known as The Goose Girl, as each year she would wait at the door of the roundhouse watching for the return of the geese. Her geese. When she saw them she would run along, chasing them, joining in with their song as they in turn joined in with hers.

In time the girl became a woman. She had children of her own and they, in turn, had children, and so on, down through the ages of time. Until the land changed and the people no longer planted by the light of the moon, nor listened at the doors for the sounds of the returning geese. Lives change. Time goes on. No one waited at the edge of the flat lands for the return of the geese.

The land that had changed. Towns and cities grew and covered the ancient pathways. Tall stone buildings now stood where, once upon a time, roundhouses were.

The mist engulfed the land in a cloak of invisibility.

Some could see through the mist. Shades of times long ago.

Annie could see. She had been able to see all her life. As a child she would run to the edge of the fields, along paths that only she could see. She would wait each year for the return of the geese. Her heart would lift with joy when she heard their song and she would raise her own voice to join theirs. Annie became known as the Goose Girl.

Annie could remember. She had memories and dreams of another time and place. Memories of another people. People who had walked these lands many years ago. Annie talked to them as she wandered the fields, seemingly alone. A solitary figure walking the green roads amongst the fens. At times the mists closed around Annie as she walked, engulfing her in a cloak of invisibility. Annie never stumbled or became lost, because she knew this place. Knew it from afar, in her dreams.

Men and women came into Annie's life. She even had a child. A daughter. Annie named her Sarah. She brought her up alone. The man was only with Annie for a season. Enough time though for him to plant a seed deep inside Annie, by the light of the full moon. The child was born as the first geese arrived.

Annie is old now. The strange woman who lived alone at the edge of the fields. The woman who walked the paths and lanes, talking to those only she could see. She was well cared for by her neighbours, food was left for her, she was always warm. Her daughter Sarah lived and worked many miles away, but would visit often, bringing her own daughter to see Annie. Her granddaughter. Light of her life. Annie called her neighbours her tribe. They were kind to her, company for her on long winter nights when the mist rolled over the fields, engulfing all in a cloak of invisibility. Annie would let them know when she needed time to herself, time when she would stand and wait for the geese, listening for their song. When she would raise her voice to join them in their song.

Annie heard the calling home song. She heard it late one winter afternoon when the geese were flying high overhead.

Annie died at the start of winter. She was found as the mist rolled away from the fields. She was laying on the ground. Her brilliant blue eyes open to the sky. A single white goose feather lay across her breast.

Earth Talk

By Jo Moscrop

I am the light, I am the breath, I am the heart of you all
I hold you every day, I bathe you with fresh waters
Into my arms you die, I take you and caress the aged years
I have loved you, and always will

You walk my paths, you sit and gaze at that which I create
Forever more you will live because of me
Why then do you hurt and scold?
The scars you create deep, deep they go, into my soul
I have loved you, and always will

When you are sad, I send the rain to kiss away your tears
When you are scared, I send the sun to shine upon you
Yet still you do not notice me
I have loved you, and always will

Please hear me when I send the wind to tell you my pain
Feel my fear when I shudder under your feet
See how you hurt me when I cry and the waters rise
I have loved you, and always will

The wild ones know, they understand
Yet even through them I cannot reach you
The pain spreads and hurts them too
Listen to the wild ones they will show you the way
I have loved you, and always will

Fighting, killing, destroying all things, will you never learn
Death, Destruction, Decay, my beautiful lands black shards

Anger, Greed, Power, all these things I do not understand
Why must you carry on this way?
I have loved you, and always will

The Great Eagle

By Asha Clearwater

There once lived a boy called Anchuk. Anchuk lived in a little village by a stream with cattle and birds and lots of laughter.

He loved his village and he loved his family. Anchuk loved to spend time with his father, listening to the breeze and the messages in it. His father taught him how to interpret those messages and how to hunt and fish, how to watch the bear and find the biggest salmon to bring home to his family.

At home his mother and his sister would prepare the fish and the skins from the animals, using them to keep them warm in the coldest of winters.

For many years Anchuk lived a happy, contented life. But one day death arrived in the village. Anchuk's father was taken with a fever and died a few days later.

Anchuk and his family were heartsick. They thought of all the wonderful things Anchuk's father had taught them, how he'd shared his thoughts with an open heart, and they smiled and rejoiced.

Although they mourned him, they also celebrated his spirit. They danced and sang and hunted and Anchuk gave thanks for the large deer he and his fellow tribesmen brought home. The deer who'd offered his life fed the whole tribe. All the village turned out to offer prayers and gifts to Great Spirit and ask him to guide Anchuk's father on the next stage of his journey.

Weeks, months passed and Anchuk continued to do the things he'd always done with his father, but this time alone. He hunted, went to the river to fish and told stories around the fire, remembering his father with love.

Some days Anchuk would go to the great mountain, climb to the highest part where the great eagle flew and pray. Pray for all his family, his ancestors, his spirit family and the many teachings he received.

One day, when the sun was at its highest point and he lay on the mountain peak, looking out over the village, he noticed a movement in the shadows.

He clutched his spear and instinctively went to throw it when a voice stopped him.

'Anchuk,' the voice said and out stepped one of the young tribeswomen from the village. He hadn't seen her down by the river for a while, but hadn't given it much thought until now.

The young girl was 16, a few years younger than Anchuk. She moved slowly towards him and then he saw her gnarled leg, twisted and contorted.

Eyes lowered, she inched forward and covered her leg with embarrassment.

'I mean you no harm. I like to stay a while and watch Great Eagle soar above the clouds, hoping he will give me a message,' she said.

He smiled and asked her to sit down with him.

They talked and talked about Great Eagle, Mother Earth, the village and the stream where Anchuk used to hunt with his father.

Anchuk spoke of his father, his eyes filling with tears and love and Vissa, the girl, smiled in acknowledgement.

They talked so much that they didn't notice Grandfather Sun bidding farewell and Grandmother Moon casting a beautiful, pure light over them.

It was only when Pathfinder Wolf howled that they stopped, looked around them and noticed the darkness.

Anchuk knew it was forbidden by the chief to be out after dark without permission.

Gathering his spear, Anchuk and Vissa ran back down the mountain, tripping over rocks in their haste to return to the village.

As they reached the edge of the camp, they fell silent, as silent as the owl that swoops, but they were not quiet enough.

One of the chief's men had seen them. 'What are you doing?' His cold, icy stare pierced right through Anchuk's heart and his blood froze.

'I, we...' he stammered, his voice weak and full of fear.

'This woman has been banished from the village,' he said. 'She has shamed her family. Why do you bring her back here?'

'I did not know,' Anchuk stammered. 'We were sitting watching Eagle on the Great Mountain and then it grew dark,' he tried to explain. 'We returned as soon as we noticed Grandmother Moon in the sky.'

The words seemed to anger the tribesman and his eyes grew black with hate.

'Leave me,' said Vissa. 'I have shamed my family. I fell in love with another man's wife and hurt all those around me,' she continued, her eyes filling with tears.

The chief's tribesman walked towards her. 'You and your kind are not welcome here. Go, leave this place or we will find other ways of punishing you.'

The girl turned and walked away and Anchuk looked on, watching her limp into the distance and blend into the landscape once more.

His heart felt sad, but he was scared and said nothing to stop the girl from leaving.

'Now, back to your hut, quickly,' said the tribesman.

Anchuk returned to his home, but his heart felt heavy, as heavy as if one of the stone people themselves were tugging at it.

He couldn't put the image of Vissa out of his head and thought of her fending for herself in the mountains.

Anchuk tried to carry on as normal. Days, weeks went past. He hunted fish and deer, even helped bring down another great member of the deer clan, with thanks for its sacrifice.

Sometimes he left a little of the meat in a pot near the

mountain in the hope that Vissa may find it. But he was too scared to go back and challenge the tribesman or visit the mountain again where Vissa sat with Great Eagle for fear of being banished from the village too.

Nothing felt the same. Even when he sat around the fire listening to stories, his heart still felt heavy.

He started to notice the way that the tribesman who had challenged him that night bullied the other younger members of the tribe. How he poked them with sticks when he thought no-one was looking or stole their knives and hid them on the edge of the village so no-one, only he, could find them.

For weeks Anchuk watched this man, saying nothing as his mind replayed the time he'd spent with Vissa and the wonderful conversations they'd had.

Then, one day, when Anchuk was sitting quietly by the river waiting for salmon to come his way, he saw the man who had sent Vissa away with a heart as cold as stone.

The man did not see Anchuk as he was lost deep in thought, looking out across the water on the other side of the river.

Anchuk waited and listened. The man let out a cry of the Great Eagle and hid in some reeds.

Suddenly soaring high above them, the Great Eagle appeared, catching golden beams of sunlight on his outstretched wings.

The eagle's beauty took Anchuk's breath away. Anchuk's heart lifted, his eyes wet with tears as he watched Eagle in all his majesty.

But just as Anchuk was about to give thanks the tribesman appeared. Lifting his bow and arrow he fired at Eagle. The arrow shot straight and true, piercing the great bird's heart, and down, down he fell until he collapsed dead at the tribesman's feet.

'No,' Anchuk cried and came running out of his hiding place.

The tribesmen looked down at the beautiful bird and smirked.

'I've wanted this bird dead every day since it soared above

my wife and that woman as they lay together, and now it is done. How could she love this ugly creature instead of me?' he said, his voice cold as ice.

Anchuk began to speak, his spear ready in his hand as his heart felt the burden of this beautiful bird's death.

But before a word was uttered he heard the pitiful scream of the tribesman – a harsher sound he had never heard before from a two legged.

Startled he looked in front of the man and there laid before him was the body of a beautiful woman, her long, black hair cascaded around her shoulders, her eyes staring into the distance.

Through her heart was the arrow, the same arrow he'd used to shoot the Great Eagle from the skies.

Anchuk looked at the man, wracked with grief, then turned and walked away into the mountains with an open heart, leaving his village behind him.

The Wildfowler's Tale

By Tony Richardson

I've lived here all my life, as my father did before me. We've got a cottage, just two rooms – eating and sleeping. We've a little land where we keep some chickens. The geese graze the common, where some of the neighbours keep a pig or two. I say neighbours – no-one's very close. The land here is close to the river, and very flat and tends to be boggy, so there aren't many places where you can build.

I make my living from the river, and the marshes, catching the fish and wild fowl. Some we cook and eat; the others we take to market where we barter them for grain and vegetables with the farmers who are on the solid ground over there, to the east.

It's not an easy life; I have to work hard, but that's no different from everyone else – the farmers work hard as well. What keeps us alive is my skill at catching the birds and fish, at knowing where they are at the different seasons and how to catch them. Not catching all of them, not taking the babies and making sure a balance is kept.

I'm a free man, not tied to the land and a lord like a villein. I'm answerable only to God, through the priest, and to my neighbours, to be neighbourly. Any disputes we settle amongst ourselves.

And now, the Bishop wants to bring all this to an end. They say they own the land, and they're going to spend money to drain it – no more fish, no more wild fowl, no more living. Where did they get the money from, I'd like to know. I've given money to the church to pay for God's work, but this doesn't seem like God's work, depriving honest men of their livelihood. They say the King said it is all right – well I've never seen him here. And what does he know about us, and our way of life?

It can't be right that outsiders, who never come here, should be interfering with our land. They don't know it, they don't respect it. They just want to make more money from it – why? Haven't they got enough? Why does anyone need more money than enough to keep his family, and put a bit by for his old age? The priest says it's God's will, and we should submit, without understanding, but he can't say how I'm to keep my family next year.

Well, they've done it. They've drained the land and I've lost my way of life. I have to work as a hireling, paid a wage, doing as I'm told, no independence, no control over what I do, no chance to put money aside, nothing to pass on to my sons. Life is no easier for me than it was before and the Bishop and the King and his men are getting richer. I'm a farmer now – well, a farm labourer. Harvesting is the hardest work, doing 16 hour days, but winter is the worst having to go out every day, whereas before I could stay snug and warm and mend my traps and nets when the weather was bad – and the birds weren't there anyway. Progress – don't talk to me about progress. It's just more for the rich, and less for the poor. And those who are supposed to look after our interests just line their own pockets. Bah!

Story Afterword by Tony Richardson

This is a true story, and elsewhere in the country would be told by those dispossessed by the Enclosures. In both cases the land was made more productive, but the benefits went to those who already had money, not those who didn't. It's not a political story – it's a story about what happens when we don't respect our neighbours. Or the land.

From the Author

Of all the thank-yous I have to make, the first should go to my trusted spirit guides for, without them, I would never have been able to write this book; they told me what to submit and even which publisher to approach. Days later, I had the publishing contract for my first ever book. So, thank you to Spirit, to the universe, to the all knowing forces that surround and guide us through life.

The second thank-you has to be for you, dear readers, for choosing to trust in me and read this book. If you'd like more, please do seek me out and tell me!

The next obvious one is a big, fat thank you to Moon Books and my team there. Thank you for trusting in a book-writing virgin. Thank you for taking a chance on me. Thank you for 'getting it'. You all rock!

Huge gratitude also for the wonderful people who took time out to read my book when it was only half way there and still believed in this project enough to provide wonderful endorsements, and to those amazing teachers who have encouraged me to keep on walking, even when the path was rocky. To Tolly Burkan, Sandra Ingerman, Paul Roland, Jonathan Horwitz, Chris Lüttichau, Howard and Elsa Malpas and all my other supporters too numerous to list here, thank you.

And now, on to the more personal acknowledgements. Huge thanks to my family – both blood and spirit – for supporting me through this journey. Thank you to my tribe – those of you who keep believing in me, even when I'm not sure I believe in myself. Thank you to all those wonderful people who seek me out and connect with me on Facebook, Twitter, YouTube and whichever other social media channels have popped up by the time this book is printed.

A special thank you to my mum – Chrissie – who never closed

down my psychic eye when I was a child by telling me I was being silly or imagining things. Thank you, mum, for always believing in me and for always, always telling me to get out there and do it.

Finally (because I always save the best for last), thank you to my best friend, my heartmate, my wife and partner through so many lifetimes, Asha. You are my rock. You are in the air of my lungs and the stillness between my heartbeats. You are my constant. My forever. My always. Thank you. X8

A final note to readers: if you have enjoyed this book, please do leave a review at your favourite online site for feedback – Amazon, iTunes, GoodReads etc – and, of course, do let me know – I really do value your feedback and you might even encourage me to write more!

Thank you,
Walk in truth and beauty,
Taz
xx

About the Author

Taz Thornton is a spiritual empowerment mentor, trainer, writer and craftswoman living in the ever-so-flat Lincolnshire fenlands and loving it! Although her teachings stem from shamanism and animism, she is also trained as a firewalk instructor and extreme empowerment coach and often incorporates these elements into her workshops to help people rediscover and reclaim their personal power.

Through Firechild-Shamanism.co.uk and TazThornton.com, Taz is in demand as a motivational speaker, as well as an energy healer and change facilitator; her work takes her across the UK and overseas, thanks to her 'go where I'm needed' outlook. Check her website for blogs and details of where to see her next, or find her on social media.

Taz spends her homelife with her wife, Asha, and their family of furries. They also share their lives with too many drums, rattles, flutes and didgeridoos!

Moon Books invites you to begin or deepen your encounter with Paganism, in all its rich, creative, flourishing forms.